THE SCIENCE BOOK OF WEATHER

Project Editor Laura Buller
Editor Bridget Hopkinson
Art Editor Earl Neish
Production Catherine Semark
Photography Dave King
Additional photography Pete Gardner

Printed in the United States of America

ISBN 0-15-365414-7

1 2 3 4 5 6 7 8 9 10   036   96   95   94   93   92

THE
SCIENCE
BOOK OF
WEATHER

Neil Ardley

HBJ

Harcourt Brace Jovanovich, Publishers

Orlando   San Diego   Chicago   Dallas

About the Author

Neil Ardley has written a number of innovative nonfiction books for children, including *The Eyewitness Guide to Music*. He also worked closely with David Macaulay on *The Way Things Work*. In addition to being a well-known author in the fields of science, technology, and music, he is an accomplished musician who composes and performs both jazz and electronic music. He lives in Derbyshire, England, with his wife and daughter.

Contents

What is weather?

Weather is what the air is like outside—moist or dry, hot or cold, windy or calm, sunny, rainy, snowy, or even hailing. A meteorologist, or weather scientist, studies the condition of the air. Every kind of weather— from the hottest sunny day to the fiercest hurricane—depends on three ingredients: water, wind, and heat from the sun. Together, they create an endless cycle of changing weather.

Wild winds
During a hurricane, the wind blows so strongly that it uproots trees, damages buildings, and causes severe flooding.

Weather watch
With the instruments you make in this book, you can study the weather and predict how it might change.

Tomorrow's weather
Forecasters study weather information then make maps such as this one to show the coming weather.

Seen from space
This weather satellite orbits the earth. It gathers information that meteorologists use to track weather systems.

Showing the seasons
The weather changes each season. As the earth orbits the sun, its tilt brings different places closer to or farther from the sun, and they get warmer or colder.

Do not disturb
Some animals, such as this mouse, sleep for the entire winter to escape the cold weather.

Sunbathing
This lizard is cold-blooded. It must bask in hot, sunny weather to warm its body and keep active.

⚠️ This is a warning symbol. It appears within experiments next to steps that require caution. When you see this symbol, ask an adult for help.

Be a safe scientist
Follow all the instructions carefully and always use caution, expecially with glass, scissors, and sharp objects. Never put anything in your mouth or eyes. Air pressure, humidity, and temperature may change slowly or not at all, so allow your instruments enough time to work.

Where's the wind?

Air moving from one place to another is called wind. Discover the direction of the wind by making a weather vane that points into the blowing wind. The wind often brings changes in the weather.

You will need:

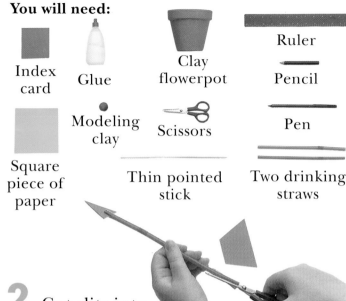

Index card

Glue

Clay flowerpot

Ruler

Pencil

Modeling clay

Scissors

Pen

Square piece of paper

Thin pointed stick

Two drinking straws

1 Cut a large triangle from the index card. Cut off the top of the triangle.

2 Cut slits into both ends of one straw. Slide the top of the triangle into the slit on one end, and the base into the other end.

3 ⚠ Push the point of the stick through the middle of the straw.

Put the hole in the flowerpot over the spot where the two lines cross.

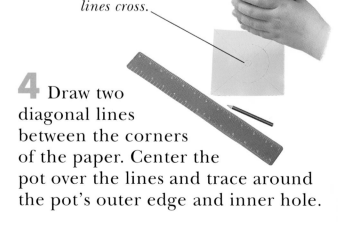

4 Draw two diagonal lines between the corners of the paper. Center the pot over the lines and trace around the pot's outer edge and inner hole.

5 Cut out the large circle, then cut across to the inner circle and cut it out, too. Turn the pot over and glue the circle to the base.

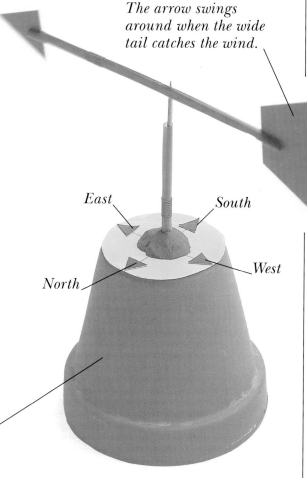

Use leftover pieces of cardboard to make pointers for each line. You may want to label them N, E, S, and W.

The arrow swings around when the wide tail catches the wind.

6 Put the other straw through the hole in the pot, sealing it in place with clay. Insert the stick. This is your weather vane.

East

South

North

West

Put your weather vane outside with the north pointer aimed north.

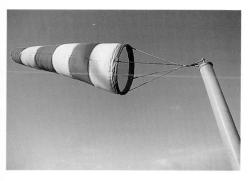

Catching the wind
Wind socks are used at airports to help pilots land and take off safely. The force of the wind raises and fills the sock, indicating the strength and direction of the wind.

Wind speed

How fast does the air move when the wind blows? Make a wind meter, or "anemometer," to measure the speed of the wind. See how the wind sometimes blows in short, strong gusts.

You will need:

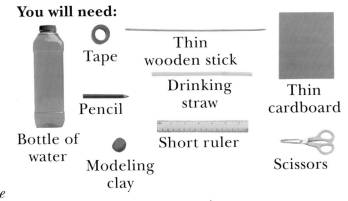

Tape

Thin wooden stick

Drinking straw

Thin cardboard

Pencil

Bottle of water

Modeling clay

Short ruler

Scissors

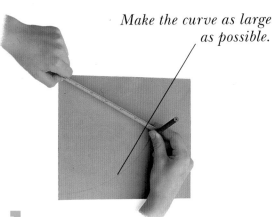

Make the curve as large as possible.

Keep the spaces between each line the same.

1 Hold the ruler in one corner of the cardboard. Then, holding the pencil at the other end, swing the ruler to draw a curve on the cardboard.

2 Draw lines from the corner of the cardboard to beyond the edge of the curve. Cut it out. This is your scale.

3 Tape the ruler to one end of the stick. Tape the straw to the cap of the bottle.

Tape the straw so that one end is just over the edge of the cap.

Tape the scale to the bottle so that the ruler hangs straight down against the scale's edge.

The speed of the wind depends on differences in air pressure—the weight of the Earth's atmosphere pushing on things.

4 ⚠ Push the stick through the straw and cover the pointed end with a lump of clay. Tape the scale to the bottle as shown.

5 This is your wind meter. The stronger—and faster—the wind blows, the higher up the scale the ruler swings.

Air moves from areas of high pressure to areas of low pressure. The greater the difference in pressure, the stronger the wind.

Spinning in the wind

Most weather stations use anemometers like this one. Its cups catch the wind, which makes them spin around. The stronger the wind, the faster the cups spin. The cups are connected to a dial that shows the wind speed.

Sun screen

How hot or cold is the air? Test its temperature with a thermometer. By screening the thermometer from the sun, you can find the air temperature.

You will need:

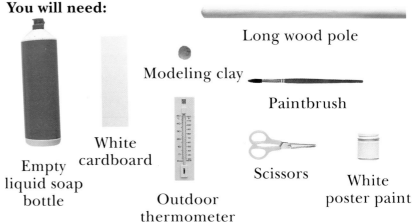

Long wood pole

Modeling clay

Paintbrush

Empty liquid soap bottle

White cardboard

Scissors

White poster paint

Outdoor thermometer

1 ⚠ Ask an adult to cut off both ends of the bottle to make a tube. Cut a hole as wide as the pole in the side of the bottle.

2 Cut the cardboard to make a shelf as wide and as long as the tube.

3 Push the hole in the tube over the wood pole and hold it in place with some clay.

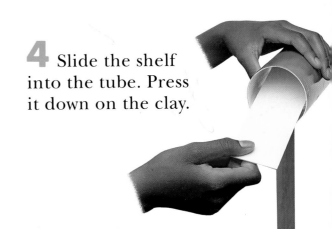

4 Slide the shelf into the tube. Press it down on the clay.

5 Paint the outside of the tube with two coats of white poster paint. This is your sun screen.

Let the paint dry between coats.

The white paint reflects, or bounces away, sunlight. Direct sunlight warms the thermometer and gives an inaccurate reading.

Air flows through the screen and around the thermometer, so the air temperature can be measured.

6 ⚠ Ask an adult to help you push the pole into the ground. Put the thermometer on the shelf. Remove it at different times of the day to read the air temperature.

You can also stand the pole up in a flower-pot filled with soil.

Taking shelter
At weather stations, thermometers and other instruments are protected from direct sunlight inside white boxes like these. Each box has slats in the sides to let air in, and a double roof that helps keep out the sun's heat.

Rain, go away

Where does all the water go after it stops raining? It "evaporates," or turns into invisible water vapor that mixes with the air. Watch a puddle disappear, and find out how the weather affects evaporation.

You will need:

Water (optional)

Wax pencil

Plate

1 Put the plate outside on a flat surface. Let it fill with rain, or pour in some water.

Use an old plate that you do not need anymore.

2 When the rain stops, draw a line around the edge of the water. Let it stand for an hour.

Daily downpour
It rains nearly every day in this tropical rain forest. The air stays damp after a rainfall because it contains so much water vapor.

3 Trace the edge of the water every hour to see how quickly the water evaporates. Try this again in different types of weather.

The rain evaporates slowly if the air is moist, and if the weather is cool or calm.

The rain evaporates quickly if the air is dry, and if the weather is warm or windy.

Water cooler

When water evaporates, it draws heat away from wet things so that they get cold. The amount of cooling depends on whether the air is dry or moist.

You will need:

Disposable dishcloth

Glass of cold water

Thermometer

Warm water

Rubber band

Scissors

1 Use the thermometer to find the air temperature. Then mix the warm water with the cold until the water and the air are the same temperature.

2 Cut out a small piece of cloth. Use the rubber band to attach it to the bulb of the thermometer.

3 Dip the cloth-covered bulb into the glass of water.

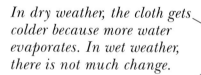

In dry weather, the cloth gets colder because more water evaporates. In wet weather, there is not much change.

4 Wave the thermometer back and forth. Then read the temperature. How much does it drop, and how cold does the wet cloth get?

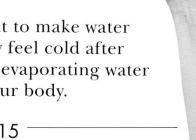

The big chill
It takes a lot of heat to make water evaporate. You may feel cold after swimming because evaporating water draws heat from your body.

Humidity tester

Can you guess if wet weather is on the way? To make an accurate prediction, you need to find out how much water vapor, or "humidity," is in the air.

You will need:

Square of cardboard

Marking pen

Blotting paper

Shoe box

Toothpick

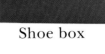
Hole punch

Strip of cardboard

Flexible drinking straw

Glue

Scissors

Pin   Modeling clay

Punch a hole in the center of each square.

1 Cut out several squares of blotting paper. Thread them onto the long end of the straw.

2 Use a lump of clay to attach the stick to the other end of the straw. This is your pointer.

If the balancing point is too close to the paper, adjust it by adding more clay to the pointer.

3 ⚠ Balance the straw on one finger. Ask an adult to push the pin through the straw at the point where it balances.

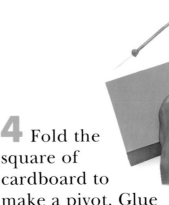

Cut two notches in the pivot.

4 Fold the square of cardboard to make a pivot. Glue it to one end of the box.

16

5 Set the pin in the notches. The straw should balance. Mark a scale on the strip of cardboard, fold the bottom, and glue it to the box. Mark the pointer's position with a dot. This is your humidity tester.

Evenly space the marks on the scale.

6 Put the tester in places with dry air and in places with damp air. The pointer rises in damp air and falls in dry air.

In damp air, the blotting paper soaks up water vapor. The paper gets heavier and the pointer rises.

When you take your tester into a place with dry air, the paper gets lighter and the pointer falls.

Places to test
A kitchen
A steamy bathroom
An attic
A cold garage
Near a heater

Opening time
Did you know that you can predict the weather with a pine cone? Its scales open up in dry air, when good weather is likely. The scales close up when the air is damp, showing that rain may be on the way.

Mist maker

Mist forms when water vapor in the air cools and "condenses," changing back into tiny drops of liquid water. This is why you can see your breath in cold weather.

You will need:

Ice cubes

Salt

Deep cake pan with dark lining

Spoon

Rolling pin

Dish towel

1 Wrap the ice cubes in the dish towel. Crush the ice with the rolling pin.

Use about a third as much salt as ice.

The air near the salted ice becomes very cold. The water vapor in your breath condenses in the cold air, forming mist.

2 Put the crushed ice in the cake pan. Cover the ice with plenty of salt and stir.

3 Wait a few minutes. Then breathe gently over the salted ice. A mist appears!

Misty morning
At night, the ground may get very cold. The water vapor in the air near it condenses and forms a morning mist.

Frosted glass

Frost often covers the trees and ground in cold weather. Where does it come from? See how frost forms by making it appear on a glass.

You will need:

Cotton swab

Spoon

Petroleum jelly

Glass

Crushed ice (see page 18)

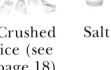
Salt

1 Dip the cotton swab in the petroleum jelly. Use it to paint a star on the outside of the glass.

2 Put the crushed ice in the glass. Cover the ice with salt and stir.

3 Wait a few minutes. A pattern of frost slowly forms on the outside of the glass.

Water vapor in the air condenses on the cold surface of the glass and freezes, forming a thin layer of ice crystals.

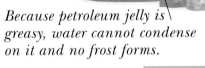

Because petroleum jelly is greasy, water cannot condense on it and no frost forms.

Wintry window
Frost can create beautiful patterns on windows. Frost is more likely to form on cold, cloudless nights, because the temperature of the ground drops more when there are no clouds.

Cloud in a bottle

How do clouds form? Find out by making a cloud appear in a bottle! A cloud is made of billions of tiny drops of water or ice crystals.

You will need:

Cold water

Matches

Drinking straw

Glass bottle with screw ca[p]

Scissors

Modeling clay

1 ⚠ Ask an adult to make a hole in the bottle cap.

Make sure the seal is tight.

2 Push the straw through the hole and seal it in place with clay.

3 Pour a little cold water into the bottle and swish it around. Then pour it out.

4 ⚠ Ask an adult to light a match. Blow it out, then hold the smoking match in the neck of the bottle so that the smoke is drawn inside.

Blow out the match close to the neck of the bottle.

Blowing into the straw raises the air pressure inside the bottle.

5 Quickly twist the cap onto the bottle and blow into the straw as hard as you can. Stop blowing and pinch the straw so no air can escape.

6 Let go of the straw. As the air rushes out, a cloud forms inside the bottle.

When you let go of the straw, the air pressure drops and the air inside becomes cooler.

The water vapor in the bottle condenses into tiny droplets, which cling to the particles of smoke and form a cloud.

Snowy summit
Clouds form high in the sky because the air pressure and temperature are lower there. The drops of water in the cloud may freeze into ice crystals, then fall to the ground as snowflakes.

Rainmaker

Before the billions of water droplets that make up a cloud can fall as rain, they must grow larger and heavier. See what happens inside a cloud to make rain fall.

You will need:

Modeling clay

Spray bottle filled with water

Cookie sheet

1 Stand the cookie sheet up on a tabletop with two lumps of clay.

Small drops of water cling to the cookie sheet and grow as other drops join them.

When a drop of water is large and heavy enough, it runs down the cookie sheet, gathering more drops as it goes.

2 Adjust the nozzle to create a fine mist. Spray the cookie sheet a few times. Some drops of water cling to the surface, but others join together and run down it.

Rainy weather
These clouds are so full of water that they block the sun. Tiny drops of water floating in the cloud clump together into larger drops, until the drops get so big that they begin to fall, and it rains.

Rain of color

Why does a dazzling arch of color form when the sun lights up a rain shower? Find out by adding a little sunshine to a bowl of water.

You will need:

Fishbowl filled with water

Black cardboard

White cardboard

As the sunlight passes through the round mass of water, it splits into the colors of the rainbow, which are reflected onto the cardboard.

1 Move a table to a sunny place. Lay the black cardboard on the table, then set the fishbowl on top.

Brilliant bow
You can see a rainbow in a rain shower if the sun is behind you. Each raindrop is a round mass of water that splits the sunlight into different colors and reflects them back at you.

2 Hold the white cardboard off to one side of the fishbowl. Hold it so that the side of the cardboard facing you is shaded. A rainbow appears on the cardboard!

Rain catcher

How much rain falls in a light shower? How much in a heavy downpour? Find out by making a rain gauge. Rain falls into the top of the gauge and collects in the bottom, where it can be measured.

You will need:

 Marbles

 Ruler

 Plastic bottle

 Scissors

 Colored tape

 Water

1 ⚠ Ask an adult to cut the top off the bottle where the width is the same as the base.

Make the bottom strip a different color than the others.

Use the ruler to place the strips about 10 mm (½ in.) apart.

2 Stick thin strips of tape on the side of the bottle. These are your scale.

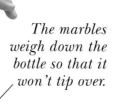

The marbles weigh down the bottle so that it won't tip over.

3 Put some marbles in the bottom of the bottle. Turn the top upside-down and tape it inside the bottle.

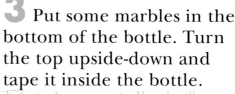

This is to weigh the bottle down so it doesn't tip over.

4 Pour water into the bottle until it reaches the bottom strip on the scale. This is your rain gauge.

Set the gauge out in the open, away from trees and roofs.

Record the total rainfall in millimeters each day. At the end of the week, pour out the rain, and refill the rain gauge to the bottom strip.

5 Put your rain gauge outside before a rainstorm. After the rain stops, see how high the water has risen.

Recording the rain
This is a rain gauge at a weather station. Rain collects in the top and drains into the drum below. If none of the rain runs off or evaporates, the depth of the water will indicate the amount of rainfall.

Bottle barometer

Air pressure can tell us what kind of weather to expect. A sudden drop in pressure usually brings stormy weather, while a rise means good weather. Test this yourself with a barometer.

You will need:

Pencil

Scissors

Tape

Thread

Paper fastener

Marking pen

Shoe box

Thin wooden stick

Long piece of spaghetti

Flexible plastic bottle with cap

1 Squeeze the air out of the bottle. Twist on the cap so that the bottle stays flat.

Make this hole halfway down the side.

Make these holes near the top.

2 ⚠ Use the pencil to make a small hole in the side of the box, and a hole in each end.

Hold the bottle in place with crushed paper, if necessary.

3 ⚠ Lay the flattened bottle in the box. Then push the stick through the holes in the box ends.

4 Knot the thread around the spaghetti. Put the paper fastener tabs around the spaghetti and through the hole in the box.

The spaghetti acts as a pointer. It should hang level and move up and down easily.

5 Gently pull the thread over the stick, and tape it to the flattened bottle.

6 Draw a scale on the box. Mark the pointer's starting position with a dot.

Rising air pressure squeezes the bottle, flattening it even more. This pulls on the thread and raises the pointer.

Falling air pressure lets the bottle expand slightly. The thread goes slack and the pointer drops.

7 This is your barometer. The pointer moves up as air pressure rises, and down as air pressure falls.

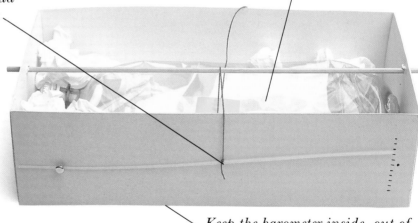

Keep the barometer inside, out of the sun and away from direct heat.

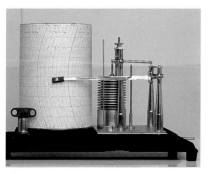

Pointing out the pressure
This barometer has a pointer that moves up and down, showing the air pressure on a chart. It works in the same way as your barometer, but uses a metal drum instead of a bottle.

What a scorcher!

Build a sunshine recorder and track the path of the sun as it moves across the sky. Your recorder works because the sun's rays are scorching hot— so be careful!

You will need:

Large flowerpot

Magnifying glass

Watering can

Aluminum foil

Colored tape

Two clothespins

Scissors

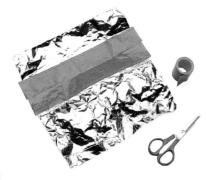

1 Tear off a wide piece of foil. Then fasten two strips of tape about 4 cm (1 ½ inches) below the foil's top edge.

2 Cut off the bottom of the foil.

You may need to tape the magnifying glass in place.

3 Use the clothespins to attach the foil to the inside of the flowerpot as shown.

4 Put the magnifying glass in the spout of the watering can.

5 On a sunny morning, position the can so that a sharp spot of light shines on the top left corner of the tape.

The sun's rays are hot enough to scorch the tape.

Adjust the magnifying glass from time to time so that the spot of light stays sharp.

10 A.M.   11 A.M.   12 NOON

When the sun goes behind a cloud, it leaves no mark.

6 A trail of scorch marks forms on the tape as the sun moves across the sky, showing when the sun shines and when it is hidden by clouds.

Seeking the sun

The glass ball in this sunshine recorder focuses sunlight on a card marked with a scale of hours. The sun's heat burns the card and makes a record of its path.

Picture credits
(Picture credits abbreviation key: B=below, C=center, L=left, R=right, T=top)

FLPA/R P Lawrence: 7CL; Geoscience Features: 25BL; The Hutchison Library: 22BL; The Image Bank/Nicholas Foster: 19BR; The Image Bank/Angelo Lomeo: 21BL; The Image Bank/Terje Rakke: 9BL; National Meteorological Library:

7TL, 13BL, 23C, 29BR; Oxford Scientific Films: 7B; Pictor International: 15BL; Planet Earth/ John Lythgoe: 14BL; Tim Ridley: 17BR; Karl Shone: 27BL; Science Photo Library: 6TR; John Woodcock: 6BR; Zefa/Kalt: 18BR; Zefa/Justitz: 11BL

Picture research Clive Webster
Science consultant Jack Challoner
Additional photography Tim Ridley

Dorling Kindersley would like to thank Jenny Vaughan for editorial assistance; Mrs Bradbury, Mr Millington, the staff and children of Allfarthing Junior School, Wandsworth, especially Daniel Armstrong, Nadeen Flower, Matthew Jones, Keisha McLeod, Kate Miller, Claire Moore, Louise Reddy, and Cheryl Smith.